The Code of the
Executive

"One who is an executive must before all things keep constantly in mind, by day and by night, the fact that he has to die."

The Code of the
Executive

Forty-seven Ancient Samurai Principles
Essential for Twenty-first Century
Leadership Success

by Don Schmincke

Charles E. Tuttle Co., Inc.
Boston • Rutland, Vermont • Tokyo

First published in 1997 by Charles E. Tuttle Publishing, an imprint of
Periplus Editions (HK) Ltd., with editorial offices at 153 Milk Street,
Boston, Massachusetts 02109.

The mask illustrated throughout this book is called a *mempo* and was
part of the traditional armor of samurai warriors.

Library of Congress Cataloging-in-Publication Data

Schmincke, Don, 1956–
    The code of the executive : forty-seven ancient Samurai principles
    essential for twenty-first century leadership success / by Don Schmincke.
      p. cm.
    ISBN 0-8048-3108-4
    1. Executive ability. 2. Leadership. 3. Management—Moral and
    ethical aspects. I. Title.
    HD38.2.S353 1997
    658.4'09—dc21   96–40262
                                              CIP

Distributed by

USA
Charles E. Tuttle Publishing
RR 1 Box 231-5
North Clarendon,VT 05759
(800) 526-2778
Fax: (800) FAX-TUTL

Japan
Tuttle Shokai Ltd.
1-21-13, Seki
Tama-ku, Kawasaki-shi
214 Japan
(044) 833-0225

Southeast Asia
Berkeley Books Pte Ltd
5 Little Road #08-01
Singapore 536983
(65) 280-3320
Fax: (65) 280-6290

First Edition
05 04 03 02 01 00 99 98 97 1 3 5 7 9 10 8 6 4 2

Design by Fran Kay
Printed in the United States of America

To my father, and other Korean War POWs,
who lived by a Code we may never fully appreciate

Contents

Acknowledgments

The preservation of this centuries-old information took efforts I can only imagine. Those I am aware of, I would like to acknowledge. First, I am humbly grateful to The Japan Foundation. As holder of the copyright to *The Code of the Samurai*, they were the source of my work and were kind enough to allow me permission to use it as the basis for this book. Second, I thank the heir to Professor A.L. Sadler's rights, the President and Scholars of St. Johns College, Oxford, for granting me permission to use his translation. Without this trail blazed, I may not have had the research to complete this journey.

This work would be far less had I not had the help of many individuals and organizations who have been instrumental in helping open my mind to new possibilities in philosophy and the nature of humankind. For their help I would like to thank the late Howard Millman, Shep Jeffreys, Wehner Erhard, Landmark Education, the Institute of Noetic Sciences (IONS), the Association for Research and Enlightenment (ARE), and the Foundation for Inner Peace and their book *The Course in Miracles.* I especially wish to thank King Jigme Wangchuk for letting a few Westerners into his majestic and humble country of Bhutan, and Inner Asia Expeditions for getting us there. It was there that the possibility of this book was born.

Updating this ancient work for the twenty-first century could be done only by rubbing elbows with those CEOs who daily engage the struggle of leadership, profits, and organizational fulfillment while never complaining of the loneliness they share. In that respect, I would like to acknowledge *The Executive Committee (TEC)*, a forty-year-old international organization of almost four thousand CEOs, for their help in letting me help others and, in so doing, learn much about the CEO experience. Special thanks to the CEOs in my TEC group in Baltimore, Maryland (in alphabetical order): Jim Abromitis, Trigen Energy-Baltimore; Chuck Buerger, Jewish Times Publishing; Mitch Diamond, Healthcare 2000; Tom Gildee, VIPS; Alan Harnik, Notes and Queries; Bill Herdrich, Poly-Seal; Mike Horne, B. F.

Joy Co.; Chip Lewis, PSA Financial; Gary Raffel, Raffel HealthCare; Brian Richardson, CSSI; Jane Satterfield, CARE Rehab; John Schock, FMS; Debbie Summers, Maryland Composition; Sudhir Trivedi, Sunbelt; and Garland Williamson, Information Control Systems. In addition, I thank the hundreds of CEOs and executives around the world who allowed me to share in their experience including Joe Ollinger, Data Services; Kim Whittemore, Bell Atlantic; Steve Carley, currently with Universal Studios; Steve Miller, Dupont; Gary Christie, Fastforms; Brian Grissler, Suburban Hospital; Atulya Mafatlal, Sungrace; Barry Gossett, Scottsman Group; Peter Monge, Montgomery General Hospital; Fran Ptak, Gascoyne Labs; Don Kirson, Kirson Medical Equipment; Alan Phillips, Phillips Corp.; Scott Schwefel, Benchmark Computer Learning; Larry Lohman, Cherrydale Glass; Dave Tate, Mercantile Bank; and the late David Richardson, CSSI. Special thanks to Diana Poss, Deb Keller, David Smith, and Eric Gundlach.

Along the path that led to this work, I met numerous individuals with whom it was a privilege to work and learn. First, I would like to thank Mike Hammer for a critical thirty seconds of coaching before I set out on my own, Richard Pascale for his books that helped me become more comfortable with a different view of business, and the author Jay

Shelov for pushing me to "get a book out." Second, I thank the outstanding colleagues who collaborated with me on various dimensions of the management journey and who, whether they know it or not, helped me translate some of the concepts in this book more effectively. They include Dan Twomey, Phil Spencer, Cathy Trower, Ric Samuels, Dick Alban, Virginia Meade, Susan Barrett, Edward Marshall and the Baltimore/Washington, D.C. TEC Chairs Richard Yocum, Bob Soady, Bill Oyler, Charlie Davis, and Les Smolin. Special thanks to Martha Peake and the American Management Association for taking the risk of publishing my first article many years ago, and giving me the confidence that led to this work, and to Patrick Ngwolo, publisher of the *World Business Review,* for allowing me some space to make a difference in the global business community.

Finally, I would like to acknowledge the individuals who contributed directly to the writing of this work. Thanks to my agent, Bob Silverstein, for taking a risk and having patience with me as this idea slowly blossomed. Also to Paul Gavazzi, who helped proof the interim draft before I locked myself in a room in Japantown, San Francisco, to complete the final one. Special thanks to Mike Knepp, who, in addition to handling our personal and corporate finances, helped me type the original translation. Of course, none of this would have been possible without my wife, Mary Zimmerman, who, after operating Zimmerman Realty daily, supported my hectic schedule with food, love, and an open ear and still had time to give me a beautiful baby girl.

Introduction

Over a thousand years ago, a group of executives set out on a daring journey. They began developing a set of principles to drive the development of their organizational leadership in a highly competitive environment. From these principles they created one of the most effective frameworks for management in history and it sustained them for seven hundred years; some claim it even set the context for their global dominance today. This book is based on what they discovered.

These insights are needed more than ever today. Managers worldwide are faced with finding ways of coping in an increasingly competitive world where markets and profits are under constant threat. More importantly, executives affect people, society, and the environment more than lawyers, doctors, accountants, the military, or any other professional group—yet they are the only ones without a code. While many seek answers and guidance in the latest management trends, there is much to be learned from an obscure ancient text that, until 1941, had not revealed its secrets to the West. It is not the first time such a text has been found to offer valuable insights for modern management. *The Art of War,* written by the brilliant military strategist Sun Tzu, has caused a recent stir in management even though it has been used by armies and politicians worldwide for over two thousand years. As an effective resource for developing corporate strategy, hundreds of books and articles have been published on this short treatise. Unfortunately, research shows that many fail to successfully apply these strategic insights, and even the effectiveness of strategic planning itself has been called into question. The strategy expert Mintzberg writes, "A number of biased researchers set out to prove that planning paid, and collectively they proved no such thing."[1] After working with hundreds of CEOs around the world for the past fifteen years, I have found that strategies do not fail because they could not be developed but

1. Mintzberg, Henry. *The Rise and Fall of Strategic Planning.* (New York: Free Press, 1994).

because they could not be implemented. There are many books on formulating strategy, but there are few on how to create an organization where strategy can be actualized. This is a book on actualization.

The principles herein emerged from a civilization that implemented competitive strategy on a larger scale than most of our present companies. How did they do it? What can we learn from them? Their seven-hundred-year journey began in ninth-century Japan when provincial authorities, managers, and proprietors developed armed bands to defend their interests. These defense groupings became more powerful as military, political, and economic forces intertwined into a feudal system competing for the prime market—property. These were the days of the samurai—a warrior class that followed a rigid code of ethics known as Bushido (the Code of the Warrior). In these organizations the regulatory government was the shogun, the market was real estate, the CEOs were feudal barons (or *daimyos*) and the executives were the samurai. These samurai managed the daimyo's organization while relying on *The Art of War* for their corporate strategy, coincidentally just as we are trying to do today.

The insights gained during these seven centuries were compiled in the text *The Code of the Samurai*, written by Daidoji Yuzan in the sixteenth century as a formal resource for training young samurai knights. It is one of the most authentic records ever produced of the system of practical and moral training for the Japanese samurai warrior. The present volume is based upon the English translation first published in 1941 by A. L. Sadler, professor of Oriental Studies at the University of Sydney from 1922 to 1948, at which time he became professor emeritus, and also professor of Japanese at the Royal Military College of Australia. I have attempted to interpret Sadler's text for today's management context while remaining as close to the original translation as possible. This was not easy to do. First, I had to walk a tightrope between preserving the original text and yet making it applicable for today's management. When in doubt, I erred on the side of preservation, hoping readers would forgive me and find value in the intention of the principle in their own lives. Second, I apologize for the male orientation of the writing. Samurai training was for men and written in a way that makes it awkward to change. Today, however, we know it is fully applicable to both genders of executives, and I intend it to be so, especially since I learned so much from the female managers in my life. Third, Japanese language has a different structure from English, and even the elements of conversation are unique. Feeling that a logical flow, modern categorization, and modern sentence structure would add value, I took the liberty of making changes accordingly. Finally, although most of the ancient text has remarkable applicability for today's executives, as you will soon see, some rewrites were necessary because there was no easy way to correlate some of the concepts in today's language. For instance, the chapter "On the Equipment of Servants" was omitted since few servants are employed in today's society (although some employees may disagree) and replaced by extracting the principle "proving yourself" from another where it was grouped. Also, references to methods for dealing with horses, caravans, personal armor, and the like were modified appropriately for today's issues.

We are samurai of the twenty-first century. The parallels of this ancient text with today's issues are startling. But even more shocking is how much we have forgotten about the inner journey of enlightenment that drove so many to achieve so much. Our business schools, consultants, and books today fail to venture into the human essence so vital for true leadership. Forgotten is the personal journey that propelled so many leaders and warriors to greatness. If ever it is intended to be there, by the time it is strained through models, analysis, and academic language, the poetry of its truth is sadly lost. The samurai did not have these "modern advantages." They had to rely on their own humanity; something we in business were never taught. So, this is a book that drives deep into your personal philosophy. As you read, consider yourself, and if you feel a slight tightening in your stomach, a tear in your eye, or fear in your heart, then the book has accomplished its purpose. To become an effective executive, you must reawaken this journey and look inside. Enlightenment is not easy. It takes work and sometimes pain to achieve the consciousness necessary for victory. For seven hundred years ancient executives practiced these truths to achieve just that. Through the miracle of written language, it has now been passed to your hands.

The Code of the
Executive

Death—The Foundation

One who is an executive must before all things keep constantly in mind, by day and by night, the fact that he has to die. That is his chief business.[2] If he is always mindful of this, he will live in accordance with the paths of Integrity, Bravery, and Honor. He will avoid a myriad of evils and adversities, keep

2. Death may seem an unlikely topic today. Upon reflection, we arrive at a different conclusion. First, medical research clearly documents how unbalanced lifestyles, conflicting priorities, time constraints, stressful decisions, career threats, poor nutrition, lack of exercise, and smoking, drinking, and other forms of drug addiction cause the early physical deaths of executives in the field of battle. Second, the organization itself can die at any time from competitive losses. Finally, the more serious death—the death of pride, arrogance, and self-importance—is as frightening as physical death. It is evident in the destructive power and political behavior that executives exhibit as they sacrifice good business decisions to preserve themselves. This is the death most feared, and the main killer of organizations. So, an executive warrior needs to keep death firmly in mind. For leadership he will die in pride and self-importance. For growth he will die in arrogance. For life he will die in the flesh.

himself free from disease and misfortune, and moreover enjoy a long life. He will also be a fine personality with many admirable qualities. For existence is as impermanent as the dew of the evening and the frost of the morning, and particularly uncertain is the life of the executive. If he thinks he can console himself with the idea of job security or unending devotion to his family, something may well happen to make him neglect his duty to both. But if he determines simply to live for today and not be consumed by tomorrow, so that when he stands before his staff he thinks of it as his last appearance and when he looks on the faces of his family he feels he will never see them again, then will his duty and regard for both of them be completely sincere. Then his mind will be in accord with the paths of Integrity, Bravery, and Honor.

In Conversation

If he does not keep death in mind, he will be careless and liable to be indiscreet and say things that offend others. If then an argument ensues, it may be settled if no offense is taken. But if it goes unsettled, the offended will speak in secret of this event to others. Then, if he goes to a meeting without preparation, he may come up against stronger political powers, and before he knows it, his career or cherished ideas may be destroyed. Even his manager's name may be brought into it, and his family and friends exposed to reproach.

All this misfortune springs from his not remembering to keep death always in his thoughts. But one who does this whenever he is speaking to others will carefully consider, as befits an executive, every word he says and will never launch into useless argument. Neither will he allow anyone to entice him into unsuitable places where he may be suddenly confronted with an awkward situation, and thus he avoids evils and regrets.

In Health and Long Life

Executive warriors who forget about death are apt to take to unhealthy excess in food and wine and ignore exercise, so that they die unexpectedly early from diseases of the liver, heart, and immune system. Even while they're alive, their illness makes them useless to anyone. But those who keep death always before their eyes are strong and healthy. And as they take care of their health and are moderate in eating and drinking and do not ignore exercise, they remain free from disease and live a long and healthy life.

In Ethics

One who lives long in this world may develop all sorts of desires, and his jealousy and greed may increase, so that he wants what belongs to others—their positions, power, and possessions. And not being able to bear parting with what is his own, he protects his holdings and becomes just like a mere politician. But if he is always looking death in the face, a man will have little attachment to material things and will not exhibit these lustful and possessive qualities. He will become, as I said before, a fine personality.

IN MODERATION

Regarding meditation on death, there is the story of the monk Shinkai, who sat all day long pondering his latter end; this is no doubt a very suitable attitude for a recluse, but not so for an executive. For to do so he would neglect his organizational duties and the ways of Integrity, Bravery, and Honor. On the contrary, he must be busy with his affairs both public and private. But whenever he has a little spare time for himself and can be quiet, he should not fail to revert to this question of death and reflect carefully upon it. Have we not seen many fall from success because of arrogance and self-importance when they do not keep death always before their eyes? And all this is for the instruction of the youthful executive.

Personal Principles

RIGHT AND WRONG

One who is an executive should have a thorough understanding of these two qualities. If he knows how to do the one and avoid the other, then he will have attained the Way of the Executive. And right and wrong are nothing but good and evil. For though I would not deny there is a clear difference between the terms, acting rightly and doing good is difficult and is regarded as tiresome, whereas acting wrongly and doing evil is easy and amusing. So, naturally most incline to do wrong or evil and tend to dislike the right and good. But to be thus un-stable and make no distinction between right and wrong is contrary to reason. Anyone who understands this distinction and yet does what is wrong is no proper executive, but a raw and untaught person, and must be removed from the ranks to protect the organization.

The cause of wrongness and evil is a small capacity for self-control. Though this may not sound so bad, if we examine its origin, we find it arises from cowardice. That is why I maintain it is essential for executives to refrain from wrong and cleave to what is right. And it is important that they inculcate this principle into the fabric of their organization.

For example, in the matter of doing right there are three degrees. Take the case of a man who goes on a business trip and rooms with a colleague who has several thousand dollars with him. To avoid the risk of carrying it around, he deposits it in their hotel room safe without anyone's knowledge except his roommate's. Then during their stay, the colleague dies from a heart attack. With no one else's knowing about the money, out of pure sympathy and compassion and without a single evil thought, the man immediately informs the relatives and returns all the money to them. This is truly a man who does what is right.

In the second case, suppose the colleague with the money had only a few acquaintances and was not intimate with anybody. In this case, no one would know about the money he had deposited, and thus there would be no one likely to make inquiries. And if the other was not very well off, he might regard it as a lucky windfall and think it no harm to say nothing and keep it for himself. But then a sudden shame would come over him for having harbored such a polluting idea, and he would at once return the money. This is a man doing right on account of shame that proceeds from one's mind.

Then there is the case where somebody in his house, either one of his family or one of his assistants, knows about his colleague's money. Therefore, he is ashamed of what that person may think or what may be said of him in the future and so returns it. This is a man doing right on account of shame connected with others' judgment of him.

So, generally speaking, the rule for the practice of right conduct is that first of all we should feel shame from the judgment of our family and friends. Next we should feel shame at the scorn of our acquaintances and strangers. Thus, we shall eschew the wrong and do what is right. This will then naturally become a habit, and in time we shall acquire the disposition to prefer the right and dislike the wrong.

As another example, consider an ancient battle. In the way of valor, he who is born brave will think it nothing to go into battle and come under a hot fire of arrows and bullets. Devoted to loyalty and duty, he will make his body a target and press on, presenting by his splendid valor an indescribably fine example to all beholders. But on the other hand, there may be one whose knees tremble and whose heart palpitates as he wonders how he is going to manage to act decently in all this danger. But he goes on because he is ashamed to be the only one to falter under the eyes of his comrades as they advance and because he fears loss of reputation in the future. So he hardens his resolution and presses on with the naturally valiant one. Thus, though he may be vastly inferior to those born brave, after several of these experiences he becomes used to it and finds his feet. Eventually his courage is confirmed, and he grows into a warrior by no means inferior to the one born fearless.

So, both in doing right and in producing valor, there is no other way to develop these qualities than with a sense of shame. For if people say of doing wrong that it does not matter, and merely jest the coward because it does not matter either, what means will there be of disciplining this kind of person? Thus, in countries where they punish criminals in a way where no shame is felt, they incur much cost for keeping many prisoners. And the habit of good and valor is not acquired in their society. Whereas in countries who punish in a way where shame and humiliation are felt from the scorn of family, friends, colleagues, acquaintances, and outsiders, they have little crime and few prisoners. And good habits are acquired by all. The latter way is a better way.

ALERTNESS

It is most important that one who is an executive warrior should never neglect the competitive spirit at all times and in all matters. For even the least of organizations cherish the strategic ability to win customers and dominate the competition, wherein is revealed the warrior spirit of this Empire of Capitalism. These lesser organizations may not, however, be executives and may not honor the Code.

So, an executive should never stop wearing his sword of "strategic thinking"—even when he goes to the bath. And if this is so in the house, how much more necessary it is when he leaves to go into the marketplace. On the way he may encounter some young entrepreneur or older organization drunk with power who may suddenly start a quarrel with him in the market. There is an old samurai saying, "When you leave your gate, act as though an enemy were in sight." So an executive must wear the sword of "strategic thinking" in his girdle, and he must never forget this spirit of the competition. And when this is so, the mind must be firmly fixed on death. The death of an executive and his organization can come at any time, as has been seen in so many other situations. But the executive who does not maintain this aggressive spirit, even though he thinks he is a strategist, is nothing more than a politician in a warrior's skin.

LEGACY

One who is an executive should continually read business cases so that he may strengthen his character. For those works that are famous everywhere in the management press and in the sagas and stories of corporate cultures give accounts of battles with detailed descriptions and the names of those who did gallant deeds, as well as the numbers of those who fell. And among these latter, the senior executives ought presumably to have figured important in the battle, but actually they were not so conspicuous for their valor, and so their names are not recorded. Even among the junior executives, only those whose valor was preeminent have been selected, and their names inscribed for posterity.

It is important, however, to realize that both the fallen who left no name behind and those whose exploits are famous through the ages felt the same pain when their heads were cut off by the enemy. So consider this well. When he has to die, the aim of an executive should be to fall performing some great deed of valor that will astonish both friend and foe alike. Thus, his death will be regretted by his CEO, and he will leave behind a great name to the generation to come. Very different is the fate of the coward who is the last to charge and the first to retire and who, in an attack on the stronghold, uses his comrades as a shield against the enemy. Struck down, he falls and dies a dog's death and may even be trampled underfoot by his own side. This is the greatest disgrace for an executive and should never be forgotten, but pondered over earnestly day and night.

COOPERATION

An executive who is in service may well have among his acquaintances or comrades one with whom for some reason he does not wish to associate. But if he is ordered to serve with such a one, he should immediately go to him and say, "I am ordered to serve with you and, though we have not been on speaking terms, I trust you will cooperate with me so we can carry out our duties properly without any difficulties." And should the other be his senior in office, he should ask him for the benefit of his kind instruction. If the day after, he is transferred to some other position, then they may revert to their former terms. Meanwhile, their agreement to work together cordially in their official duties is the correct conduct for an executive.

How much more between comrades who have no such impediment should there always be the most hearty mutual cooperation when they are serving together. But those who are always striving for power may not cooperate with others. Lacking kindness of heart, they will not give assistance to those new to office and unacquainted with its details. They will not help them to function efficiently and will even rejoice when they make mistakes. These types of people show a nasty mean spirit and are entirely worthy of censure. This is the sort of executive who will do some dirty trick like turning against his own side when he finds himself in an awkward situation. So, anything of the kind is to be strictly avoided.

Self-Worth

In ancient times when speaking of someone's income, executives would say that a man was hardly able to keep a spare horse, when they meant he had a substantial income. Or that one could just afford to keep a half-starved beast if he had marginal income.

Similarly, substandard income was described as allowing a man to have one rusty spear. For up until then the ancient style of executives still survived, and it was not their way to mention figures to describe someone's income. They used these expressions because a man's worth was not based upon his amount of income, and no one was shamed for having less than another. "A hawk may be starving but he won't touch corn" and "The samurai may have eaten nothing but he uses his toothpick" are sayings that illustrate this sentiment.

Young people then never spoke of personal profit or loss or mentioned the price of anything. And they would blush if they heard any talk of love affairs. Today's executives sometimes confuse a man's worth, or their own, with the size of his house, type of car, style of dress, thickness of wallet, or even whether he owns boats or planes. This is a tragic confusion. It distracts from the essence of life and of executive duty. Though today's executives may not reach the ideals of the ancients, all should admire and study them. The samurai would say, "Though a man's nose be crooked, if he can breathe through it, all is well." This is the way we should regard it.

INTEGRITY

One who is an executive should base his conduct on

a strong sense of integrity, especially as it pertains to family duty and social responsibility. However capable, eloquent, and handsome one may be born, if he has no integrity, he is of no use at all. For the Way of the Executive requires a man's conduct to be correct in all points, and his actions to follow his words at all times. If there is no discrimination in all matters, there will be no knowledge of what is right. One cannot be randomly selective in taking "right" action. One cannot act in business differently from how he acts in family life or society. One cannot be a thief in the night and not in the day. One cannot be a liar in social settings, but not one in a boardroom. All actions in all situations must be considered right. Otherwise, the integrity of the executive is in question. And one who does not know what is right can hardly be called an executive.

For instance, an executive with this complete insight realizes that his parents are the authors of his being and that he is part of their flesh and blood. Now in rendering filial obligation to parents there are two types of people. The first is where the parents' disposition is honest, and they educate their children with sincere kindliness. They leave them all their property, finances, furniture, and household treasures, as well as accepting their marriages. When such parents retire, it is neither praiseworthy nor remarkable that their children should look after them with all consideration. Even toward a complete outsider, if he is an intimate friend and goes out of his way to be helpful to us, we feel very kindly disposed and shall do anything we can for him, though it may be contrary to our own interests. How much deeper then must the bond of affection be between parent and child? However much parents do for their children, they cannot but feel it is never really quite adequate. And this is just the ordinary filial piety that is not anything remarkable.

But what if the parents are not kind but old, crotchety, and always nagging, insisting that they deserve all that belongs to them? And what if they give their children nothing, yet always make constant demands for attention? And whenever they meet others, they complain of unfilial children and the discomfort they have in their old age, thus giving their children a bad name among outsiders? Even such cantankerous parents must be revered as parents, their bad tempers appeased, and their aged infirmities handled without showing any signs of annoyance. For exerting oneself to the utmost for such parents is real filial piety.

An executive who possesses this spirit when he enters the service of an organization will thoroughly understand the Way of Integrity and will show it not only when the management team is prosperous but also when it meets adversity. And this person will not leave when one barrier becomes ten, and this ten a hundred, but will support it to the last, regarding his personal agenda as nothing in carrying out a warrior's fealty. And so the terms "parent" and "organization," "filial conduct," and "integrity," are distinct.[3] They are in no way different in meaning. There is a saying of the ancients, "Look for a loyal retainer among the filial"; and it is unreasonable to think that if a man is unfilial to his parents, he can at the same time be loyal to a team. Or if a man demeans another, he can at the same time be trusted to support his colleagues. For if anyone is incapable of carrying out his filial duties to his parents from whom he sprung, it is very unlikely that he will give committed service to an organization of people who are of no relation, out of pure gratitude or compensation. Or if he is incapable of honoring his word to another outside the department, it is unlikely that he will have integrity inside the department. When he enters an organization, an unfilial son of this kind will be critical of any shortcoming of his manager. And when he does not approve of any-

3. With today's extended lifestyle, and with children leaving home to remote locations, the honor and duty to parents have become blurred. Ancient Asian customs may not be directly translated everywhere, but the point is still relevant: How one treats others—family or strangers—is an indicator of how he will behave inside the organization. This is not to be taken lightly when we realize that although most employees are hired for skills and experience, the majority of firings are due to behavior. Behavior should therefore be a priority in hiring.

thing, he will throw off his allegience and slip away at a critical moment or betray his team by giving himself up to the enemy. There are examples of such disgraceful conduct in all periods, and it is to be shunned with abhorrence.

BRAVERY

For the Way of the Executive, the three qualities of Integrity, Bravery, and Honor are essential. We speak of the executive with integrity, the bold executive, and the righteous executive, but it is he who is endowed with all three of these virtues who is of the highest class. Unfortunately, among the myriad of executives, it is rare to find one of this kind. Now the executive with integrity and the righteous executive may not be difficult to identify by their ordinary, everyday conduct, but it is not so easy to single out the bold one in stable times—anyone is a good captain in a calm sea. But it is the bold one who is most valuable in times of corporate crisis or when sustained innovation is essential to keep enemies at bay.

It is not necessary, however, to wait until a crisis to discern who is brave, for bravery does not show itself first when a man puts on armor and goes into battle. You can see whether he has it or not when he is leading his ordinary life. For he who is born brave will challenge the CEO when appropriate.

He will not flatter his superiors and will boldly state what is right.[4] He will take risks for new and exciting changes. Whenever he has any leisure time, he will use it for study, and he will not be negligent in practicing the management arts. He will be on his guard against indolence and will be very careful how he invests his money as well as his time. If you think this shows detestable stinginess, you will be mistaken, since he spends freely where it is necessary. He does not do anything that is contrary to the principles and values of the culture of the organization, however much he may wish. He preserves his life in the hope of someday doing a deed of outstanding merit. He can be found moderating his appetite for eating and drinking, and avoiding overindulgence in pleasures so that he may preserve his body in health and strength. For in these, as in all other things, it is rigid self-control that is the beginning of valor.

But he who is not brave, on the other hand, will appear to be only superficially supportive of his CEO, without any sincere intention of remaining so. He will be in constant agreement even if the CEO's

4. CEOs agree that when they assumed their role it was the last time they got a straight answer. People do not like telling their superiors bad news. CEOs need to be cautious not to encourage this or "shoot the messenger"—extremely cautious. Toward the end of its successful growth, IBM had a philosophy of "If you can't give me good news, I'll find somebody who can!" Certainly a macho attitude was of great importance to a lot of impressed IBMers. The only problem is, everybody got good news. Most executives never knew there was a problem until they had to fire almost half the workforce.

ideas are not good. He will not challenge his superiors or his colleagues unless it is to his own benefit to do so. Indifferent to the principles and values of the organization, he is given to probing where he should not be, doing what ought not be done, and, in everything, putting his own inclination first. He particularly dislikes having to study the management arts but acts like he knows all about them. He reads the latest management books and thinks he is an expert but disdains to practice what they teach. He is found merely boasting about his past skills, his self-importance, his connections, and all manner of things that can be neither substantiated nor believed. He spends any amount of money on luxuries without the least foresight. But where he ought to spend, he is stingy and will not even share in buying his round of drinks when it is his turn. He eats and drinks too much, and is excessive in pleasures, and his health is too poor for him to serve the organization properly. This sapping of his physical powers and longevity is due to nothing but a weak and untutored mind incapable of self-control. And he has no consideration for the trouble and anxiety this causes his family. We would not be far wrong in diagnosing a source of cowardice in this executive. And so can the brave and valiant be distinguished from the coward, even during peaceful times.

HONOR AND RESPECT

The Ways of Integrity, Bravery, and Honor are not limited to executives. They are equally incumbent on all classes of employees, customers, and the competition. But sometimes these classes may do things that are impolite or disrespectful. They may even show lack of respect by using the company name in an unflattering way and by causing wrong views to be expressed. For an executive, however, it is different. No matter how truthful and honorable he may say he is, if he is lacking in the correct manners and etiquette with which respect is shown, he cannot be regarded as living in proper conformity with it. Any negligence of this kind is no conduct for anyone who desires to be an executive. Even when out of sight, there must be no relaxation in Integrity, Bravery, and Honor.

With the CEO and senior management, an executive must at all times maintain a respectful attitude, just as these executives maintain respect for their subordinates. Anger or unkind words should not be said, and should contrary opinions need to be voiced, they should be said firmly and with conviction. Any agreement or disagreement should be honored and not used as evidence to express disrespect about the company or its management. It is better for an executive to leave and be of service elsewhere than to damage the house whose name is on his card.

When dealing with employees, respect is essential for professional and honorable action. An executive must respect employee opinions, feedback, and argument even if they do not agree with his own views. Employees are the frontline, and their empowerment and performance is directly related to the respect they feel. Good leaders already know this. Poor leaders try to preserve their power and status so that they may achieve their greatness at the expense of the employee. To the poor leader, power over the employee is more important than making them powerful. This is the utmost in disrespect. This type of executive must be removed for violating the Code and to prevent further damage to the commitment of the employees.

This attitude must also extend to the treatment of customers, the competition, and the Earth. It is a show of stupid lack of consideration when one speaks ill of any of these. Customers are the source of being for the corporation and should be respected, as the Earth should be respected as the source of life. The competition should be respected in that disparagement and ill comments only make the executive look cowardly and incompetent. Winning customers from the competition should be done on the corporation's own merits. Though the competition may fight as unskilled warriors and may not even honor the Code, there is no excuse for an executive to compromise his values.

THRIFT

Executives who are in service, both great and small, must always practice thrift and have the discrimination to do it so they do not have a deficit in their household expenditure. As to those with a large income, if they find they are living beyond their means, they can quickly make a change in their affairs by saving here and cutting down there. Thus, they can soon recover their solvency because they have a certain surplus. But if he with a small income tries to live like a rich executive, he incurs unnecessary expense and gets into difficulties. He cannot recover, because he has nothing to fall back on, and however much he tries to economize, he only becomes more indebted until at last he comes to complete ruin. Since people's domestic affairs are a private matter, and one in this situation must incur certain necessary expenses, he will be driven to every possible trick and device, even to saying what should not be said and doing what should not be done. For it is financial difficulty that induces even those with a high reputation to do dishonest things that are quite alien to them.

One must make a firm resolve to live only

according to one's means and be very careful not to indulge in any useless expenses. He must spend money only on what is necessary, for this is what is called the Way of Economy. But about this there is one thing that must be noted. To do nothing but talk about economy and not spend anything, saving and skimming everywhere and being delighted when you can add one coin to another by some tightfisted trick, is to acquire a mentality devoted to filthy lucre. Eventually one will lose all sense of decency as to do what ought not be done and leave undone what should be done. People of this type lose all instincts except that of hoarding, and what they practice is miserliness, not economy. Stinginess in an executive is to be abhorred. For if he puts all the money there is before duty and grudges to spend it, how much more will he grudge risking his precious career for the changes necessary for organizational vitality? That is why those of old in China said that stinginess is regarded as synonymous with cowardice.

FRIENDS

For an executive who is in service to an organization, it is most important that he associate with and make great friends of only those among his colleagues who are valiant, dutiful, wise, and influential. But as men of this kind are not very numerous, he may find only one among his various friends on whom he can thoroughly rely in time of need. Generally speaking, however, it is not desirable for an executive to make a great friend of someone whom he prefers to eat, drink, and socialize with. For if he discovers a kindred spirit and makes a great friend of him, thinking he will be an amusing companion, they may easily come to behave in a manner quite unsuitable to their class—treating each other without ceremony, sprawling up against each other, spending their evenings bawling songs and ballads, and using too familiar terms of address. They may appear most intimate one moment and then, from insistence on some trifle, fall out and not be on speaking terms the next. Such contemptible want of dignity shows unprofessionalism and may allow staff to politically manipulate this friendship for their own ends.

If such great friends are social companions, poor judgments may result because of personal interests conflicting with business ends.[5] Similar to family relations in a business, a great friend should in no way compromise or want to compromise the Code of another. Yet if the friendship is intimate, such a conflict may occur.

---

5. Intimate friendships may cause problems if they hinder objective decisions necessary for the good of the business. For instance, the "good ol' boy" network recently frustrated a banking executive client when he tried to save 20 percent in property-management costs with a new supplier. He was told not to do it because "Jack went to prep school with me. He's a good guy. He's one of the blue-blood families." The bank now loses hundreds of thousands of dollars from a personal decision to keep an incompetent vendor.

Reliability

Reliability is one of the qualities of the Way of the Executive, but it does not mean that he should offer assistance or go along with a plan without special reason. Neither should he put himself forward in things that do not matter or take upon himself obligations in affairs that do not concern him, just for the sake of doing so. Even in things that do concern him to a slight extent, it is much better to be aloof if no one asks him to interfere. Because even small questions, let alone more complicated ones, if an executive becomes implicated in them, may involve him so that he cannot withdraw without risking his precious career, which should be at the disposal of the CEO. Therefore, I say that he should not be needlessly obliging.

If a samurai of former days was asked a favor, he would consider whether it was one that could be granted or not. If the latter, he would decline at once. And if he did entertain it, he would undertake it only after careful thought, so that he was quite prepared to deal with it quickly so the whole affair soon could be settled. In consequence, the supplicant's difficulties were resolved and the benefactor gained great praise. If, on the contrary, without this reflection he takes upon himself some responsibility that he is unable to carry out properly, he will gain a reputation for being unprincipled when this becomes apparent.

Giving one's advice or opinion should be done only after mature consideration. For though parents, teachers, elder brothers, uncles, and so on may give unsuitable advice to their children, pupils, and nephews without much harm, everything that comes out of the mouth of an executive must be cautious and guarded. Particularly to his friends and colleagues must he be most judicious in his utterances. When he is singled out and asked to take part in a consultation, he may of course say he has no views on the subject and refuse to discuss it. But if he does become a party to the discussion, he will be most helpful if he states exactly what he thinks, clearly and succinctly without reserve and without regard for the disapproval or resentment the others may show. For if out of weakness or fear of offending them, he exhibits a hesitancy and turns aside from what is just and agrees with what is not reasonable and, in order to avoid a rupture, allows unsuitable things to be said and burdens to be laid on others, then he will eventually be voted a futile counselor and reviled and despised. On the other hand, if anyone is so stupid as to think himself too important to ask for advice, arguing that there is no need of consultation and wishing to decide everything according to his own opinion, he may make a mess of things. In this case he will likely find himself not very popular among his fellows as a result.

ACCOUNTABILITY

An executive in service, as I said in the first chapter, must be one who lives for today but cares nothing for tomorrow. If this is so, and he does what he has to do day-to-day with zeal and thoroughness so that nothing at all is left undone, he has no reason to feel any reproach or regret. But living in the moment of the day does not mean ignoring future consequences. Troubles arise when people rely on the future and become lazy and indolent and let things slide. They put off quite urgent affairs after a lot of discussion, not to speak of less important ones, in the belief that they will do just as well the next day. They push off this responsibility onto one comrade and blame another for shortcomings. And when trying to get someone to do something for them, if there is no one to assist them, they leave it undone, so that before long there is a big accumulation of unfinished jobs. This is a mistake that comes from relying on the future against which one must be very definitely on one's guard.

For instance, on whatever day of the month you have to go to a meeting, you must calculate the time it will take you to travel there from your office and allow for this length of time so that you are ready just a little before the actual hour of the meeting. Some silly fellows waste time by having a smoke or chatting with their secretaries and colleagues when they ought to be starting, and so leave their office late. They then have to hurry so much that, as they walk or drive, they do not acknowledge with courtesy people they pass. And when they do get to their destination, they are all covered with perspiration and breathing heavily, and then have to make some plausible excuse for their lateness on account of some very urgent business they had to do. When an executive has a meeting, he never ought to be late for any private reason. And if one man takes care to be a little early and then has to wait a bit for a comrade who is late, he should not sit down and yawn, neither should he hurry away when his time is up as though reluctant to be there. For these things do not look at all well either.

HUMILITY

An executive who has done some special service for his CEO and considers it something extraordinary, and perhaps others think so too and praise him, should understand that the matter may not appear quite the same to the CEO himself. Even if the CEO does feel moved inwardly, there may be something else about it that offends him. And so if the executive does not get any recognition and thinks his merit is overlooked, he may be dissatisfied and show how he feels by complaining continually about his CEO's ingratitude. This is, it need hardly be said, the error of one who does not appreciate what service is.

Now the samurai of the civil war period were in the field innumerable times in their day and risked their lives freely for their lords and commanders, but they did not talk about their merit or their valiant deeds. Today's executives, however, can be found merely shuffling about their desks, rubbing the backs of their hands, and fighting battles with three inches of tongue. This is certainly nothing like risking one's life in war. But in both cases, it is the duty of executives to serve in just the same spirit of loyalty. And whether what they do is anything special, praiseworthy or not, is for their CEO to judge. It is enough that they resolve to do their duty properly. They are not to be called upon to express any feelings of discontent.

AVOID RUMOR AND SLANDER

An executive who is in a company's service must always be very careful not to indulge in the underhanded rumor of any faults of his comrades that he may come to hear of or see. For a man cannot calculate how far he may have unwittingly mistaken or misunderstood these things. Moreover, since senior executives are the channel for the wishes of the CEO, any criticism of them is a reflection upon him. Then again, you may someday have to approach one of them with an urgent request or to humbly ask their favor. To suddenly have to change your tone when just before you had been slandering him behind his back is the kind of thing no executive ought to bring himself to, however weighty the business.

AVOID BRAGGING [6]

In ancient days there were many who had the reputation for being braggarts among the samurai. In fact, in those days every daimyo was likely to have several samurai who were of this type. They were men with many great exploits to their credit and in no way deficient in the Way of the Warrior, but on occasion apt to be obstinate and difficult. And when they were pressed in their living conditions and some incident arose from their income and office being incompatible with their high reputation, they would become reckless and say what they pleased without

6. This principle is so timeless, it is left pretty much intact from the original translation. The ego and pride that plague most organizations and cause the politics and empty drama we know so well are not new phenomena. It was so critical hundreds of years ago, it was a special chapter in the Way of Bushido.

any regard for their company. But their lord and the counselors and elders of their clan would overlook it and take no notice. So, they became more and more belligerent and would tell anyone what they thought of their good or bad points without reserve or apology, and so they continued to do all their days. Such were the braggarts of old, men with a record of great deeds.

But the braggarts of today are fellows who have never even put on a suit of mail and who spend most of their time sitting with their friends and acquaintances discussing the defects of their organization. They enjoy pointing out the failings of their superiors, certainly not omitting the misdeeds of their own comrades, while at the same time emphasizing their own superiority. Such shallow heads are a world apart from the brave braggarts of old and should properly be labeled as charlatans and fools.

MATTERS LITERARY, AESTHETIC, AND ATHLETIC

Though the Way of the Executive first implies the qualities of strength and effectiveness, to develop only this one side is to be nothing but a rustic executive of no great account. So an executive ought certainly to be literate and, if he has time, should take up poetry or the study of fine arts to a certain extent. For if he does not study, he will not be able to understand the reasons of things past or present. However worldly-wise or shrewd he may be, he will find himself greatly handicapped at times by this lack of learning. For if you have a general understanding of the affairs of your own country and of foreign lands and carefully consider the three principles of time, place, and position, you are not likely to make many mistakes in your calculations and will follow the best course. That is why I assume an executive should be studious. But if he makes bad use of his knowledge, grows opinionated, looks down on the illiterate, worships everything foreign, thinks he is too good for common possessions, and is so prejudiced that he cannot perceive a thing to be inappropriate for a situation, good though it may be in theory, then I say his learning is too much of a good thing. With this in mind, he should study.

Again, the humanities and arts are a custom of a civilization, and great leaders in all ages have distinguished themselves in certain areas. So, even a humble manager will do well to go for it and try his hand at clumsy music, painting, language, or some other art. But anyone who gets entirely absorbed in it and neglects his ordinary duties will become soft in mind and body and lose all martial qualities, becoming like a self-absorbed, second-rate artist. Particularly if you get too fond of an art, although fashionable, you may easily become glib-tongued, witty, and smart even in the company of grave and reserved colleagues. Though this may be amusing in society at the present time, it is an attitude executives ought to avoid.

Although modern executives in the West have not adopted the tea ceremony used by the samurai knights, they have evolved other forms of socialized business interaction in the form of sports. For example, golf, from the days of barons and tycoons, has been very much the diversion of the executive class. Even if you are not yourself a great enthusiast yet, you are likely to be invited to take part in it and be a partner with people of high degree. So, you ought to know at least how to enter the clubhouse and its precincts properly, how to make arrangements intelligently, how to select clubs, and how to score correctly. To obtain this knowledge of the rules of the game, it is advisable to take some lessons from a professional. Again, the golf course is a place very profitable for deal-making and building relationships far removed from the distractions of the office. This is so valuable that often you will find courses adjacent to the grounds of the wealthy and of businesses, set in what seems to be a solitary landscape with bare simplicity and elegant clubhouse gates and entrances. The equipment such as clubs, bags, and other accessories are equally without any gaudy ornamentation, but are of a clean and reticent form entirely eschewing the impurities of everyday life—a spirit that, if cultivated, I think is of great assistance in sweetening the Way of the Warrior. So it is no bad thing for anyone to make a place for golf in his life even if he has membership only in the lesser courses, used clubs of older design, and a worn golf bag so that all is quite inexpensive and in accordance with the austere style of a humble executive.

But in all things the simple is very apt to become complicated, and luxury may show itself, in either the arts or athletics. For instance, if when you see someone else's instruments or equipment, you feel disgusted with your own, you will soon come to want all your accessories to be things of value. Then you will cultivate an eye for a bargain and go in for connoisseurship, so that you can pick up a fine set for a small sum. If you see anything very attractive at anybody's house, you will importune him for it or else want to make an exchange for it with, of course, the intention of getting the best for yourself. This kind of thing is no better than the nature of a huckster and degrades the Way of the Warrior to that of a mere politician. It is a very bad fault, and rather than practice this kind of art or sport, it is better to know nothing about it at all and to remain ignorant of even how to hold the equipment. For it is preferable to appear a little boorish than to spoil the quality of the Way.

Roles and Responsibilities

POLITICS AND POWER

An executive in service is under a great debt to his company and employees for granting him the opportunity and leadership to retain his position. The ancient samurai may have felt they could hardly repay their lord except by committing suicide and following him in death. But this is not permitted by law. What then is left? Perhaps a man may wish for an opportunity to do something more outstanding than his comrades, to take a strategic risk in order to accomplish something great and beyond the status quo. If he resolutely makes up his mind to do something of this sort, I am sure he will agree it is a hundred times more preferable than performing suicide.

For he may become the savior, not only of his company but of all his fellow employees both senior and junior. He will thus become a legend who will be remembered to the end of time as a model executive possessing the three qualities of Integrity, Bravery, and Honor.

For example, there is always an evil spirit that haunts the executive team. The first way the spirit curses the team is by causing the accidental death or epidemic disease of some young executive who has the three virtues and who promises to be of great value in the future. This loss is therefore a severe blow.

In the second place, this evil spirit will enter into a member of the executive team whom the CEO most trusts and favors. He then becomes a political animal and deludes the CEO's mind by seducing him into ways of injustice and immorality. Now, in thus leading the CEO astray, this executive may do so in six different ways. First, he may prevent him from seeing or hearing anything and contrive that other team members cannot state their views or, even if they can, that those views are not adopted. He will generally manage the process so that the CEO regards him alone as indispensable and commits everything to his keeping.

Second, if he notices any of the executives in the company who seem promising and likely to be useful to the CEO in the future, he will have him transferred somewhere else and kept away from the executive suite. He will, through connections of his own, arrange that only men who agree with him, are subservient, and never oppose him are the only ones permitted to be around the CEO. Thus he prevents the CEO from knowing anything about the extravagant and domineering way he lives.

Third, he may persuade the CEO to take an outside interest in a project that he deems important for the future strategy of the company. He will procure consultants for this purpose without any inquiry into their integrity except that they agree with him. And he will send the CEO on trips and excursions, assuring him they are essential for his duty. Even he who is by nature clever and energetic is apt to be led astray by these consultants, much more than one who is born lacking in these qualities. Then the CEO's discrimination will depart from him, and he will think only of these amusing projects, becoming more and more addicted to them, so that eventually he will be entirely distracted day and night. He will come to spend all his time in the office, without a thought for official and administrative business and hating even the idea of an interview on these subjects. Therefore, everything remains in the hands of the one evil executive, and day by day his power increases, while all the others become mere nonentities: shrinking men with lips compressed, as the whole company goes from bad to worse.

In the fourth place, it follows that under these circumstances everything is kept secret. As expenses increase and income has to be augmented, old regulations are done away with and new ones enacted. A spy is placed here, someone is bribed there, and allowances are cut down. Employees are demoralized without anyone caring in the least about them, all so their CEO may have alternative distractions. Although they do not say anything about it publicly, the greatest discontent is rife among the executives, and before long there is none who is single-heartedly loyal to the company.

In the fifth place, though a CEO should never be anything but experienced in the Way of the Executive, the evil executive is not likely to care anything about the Way. There will be no interest at all in competitive matters and no inspections of the strengths and weaknesses of the organization. Everyone in the company will be quite pleased to fall in with this attitude, and none will trouble about duties or make proper provisions for weapons and supplies. They will be perfectly content to let things alone and just make do for the present. No one would think, seeing the condition of the organization, that their ancestors had been warriors of great renown. Should some crisis occur and find them unprepared, there would be nothing but flurry and confusion, as nobody would know what to do.

In the sixth place, when the CEO is thus addicted to his distractions, he will be stressed under the illusionary urgencies and will grow more and more wayward till his health becomes affected. All his executives will be dispirited and lacking in sincerity, merely living from one day to the next without any guidance from above. Eventually something may happen to the CEO through the influence of this evil spirit.

The evil executive who is at the bottom of it all, this vengeful enemy of his CEO and evil genius of his company, will no doubt be cursed by all the organization. Even so, there will be nothing to do unless nine or ten executives band together to accuse him and bring him to judgment by a war of argument without soiling their hands. But in that case the affair cannot be cleared up without making it public. The CEO and his company will incur bad PR, and then matters may become more serious and end in a sentence being passed upon them by the board. In all ages, when a CEO has been unable to manage his affairs and has been disciplined by the board, the result has been that his rule has come to an end. As the proverb has it, When you straighten the horn, you kill the ox, and when you hunt the rats, you burn the shrine. So it is when the CEO's house is ruined—the executives are discharged and lose their livelihood.

Therefore, it is best that you seize this great rascal who is the evil spirit of the team and cut off his head. This may be done by an end run to the board, a cunning setup that exposes his evil, a direct appeal to the CEO, or some other intervention of great risk, whichever you prefer, in order to put an end to him and his corrupt practices. And then, if a backlash is likely, you must straightaway fire yourself so that there will be no lawsuit or bad press, and your CEO's person will not be tainted. Thus, the whole organization will continue to live in security, and there will be no open trouble in the empire. One who acts accordingly is a model executive who does a deed a hundredfold better than suicide. He has the three qualities of Integrity, Bravery, and Honor and will hand down a glorious name to posterity.

SACRIFICE

When an executive is in service to an organization, his CEO may find it necessary to incur very large expenses. Should circumstances become strained, he may need to reduce salaries and bonuses of his executives for a certain number of months or years. In this case, whether the amount is great or small, it is highly improper for an executive to suggest or even hint in the privacy of his family, much less outside it, that this causes him any difficulty or embarrassment. Since the ancient samurai, it has been the custom for executive knights to accept their leadership responsibility for the state of the organization and to rally to the help of their CEO in his time of need, just as he has always been ready to help them in theirs.

When a CEO is stressed by having to meet liabilities, negotiate with creditors, and perform surgery on the balance sheet, it may affect his normal duties and prevent him from undertaking responsibilities considered his business. This can become a very painful situation for his staff to operate in. However, ordinary affairs can still be carried out, and it is the duty of the executive team to pull together and step in where leadership is missing, in order to keep the company moving forward.

This call for duty can occur at any time. Should tomorrow some unexpected competitive disturbance arise on the frontier of the market, and the organization need to defend its position, the first thing it would need is money. And however clever one may be, this commodity cannot be produced immediately. It will require sacrifice. Without it the company becomes, as the proverb has it, like a man with his hand caught under a stone who cannot move in any direction. As competitors will all be ready to start positioning themselves, and that day cannot be altered, the company cannot escape from the need to defend itself. When this happens, all executives, both senior and junior, seasoned and newly hired, must not fail to cut costs, rearrange work more efficiently, and be prepared to contribute a suitable proportion of their salaries or bonuses. During this period of reduced income, everyone has to use their brains and contrive ways to cut down the costs of doing business. These ways may include decreasing the number of steps in a work process, identifying priorities, improving productive capacity, or focusing on those things that matter in time of war. Then they should bag a lunch, type their own letters, file their own papers, answer their own phones, make their own coffee, and put up with every possible hardship. It is the duty of all who are in service to bend their energies to keep affairs in proper order. One can, for instance, do away with the new copier or settle for just an upgrade to an old PC or cut back on travel. With the value of these, the CEO could have enough without having to borrow. And if he has to borrow, these actions will please the bank and convince them to lend the money.

Even in times of market peace, we must consider all this and its importance, and a CEO should not wait to invoke this state of affairs. For if we put up with these difficulties, even in a peaceful period of economy, we can meet any special need of the business during an emergency. We can even have extra money to capture such opportunities as a conference presence, with a brave show for people from around the world as they come crowding in to see our products. Exposed to the view of all customers, if our display is inferior to others, it is a lifelong shame to the CEO and the organization.

So even if the CEO does not hear of it or other staff despise you for it, it is an unspeakable thing that an executive should be thought to make complaints about the reduction of his salary. For it is a coward who stays in the camp when times are safe and good but leaves when it becomes necessary to fight.

Call to Arms

An executive who is favored with a salary by his CEO must not consider his life his own alone. For among those who render service there are two types. There are the employees who work hard all the time but who are not necessarily bound to lay down their careers for their company. They cannot be considered culpable if they do not show themselves specially trained or skilled in the management arts. Then there is the executive. He is quite different. For he is a servant who risks his career, as the CEO does with the board, but on a different scale. Should any trouble arise in the empire, he has to render service suitable to his status. That is to say, he should apply his budget and resources, along with the number of employees under his care, according to the statutes of the board. As with the ancient samurai, when an executive has to lead his forces out to war in a market sector, he must also have a sufficient number of men left behind to protect other markets against attack. So, though he does not need them all the time, he has to maintain a sufficient number who are capable.

And in return for all this, the executive does his ordinary peacetime duty as a company officer, a commonplace sort of performance that can scarcely be called outstanding service. But there may be at any time a sudden call to arms when he must take his place in the ranks as a leader. If it is an attack on their market, he must respond as a formidable competitor. If the enemy outperforms the organization in production, he must become a process-improvement champion. If his company's quality is second best, he must act as an agent of change. In each case he may have to give his career for his colleagues under the onslaught of the foe and die a splendid death where he stands without yielding an inch. This indeed is the deepest sense of service in the executive when he steels his resolution and shouts, "God be my witness, I will show you a deed that no other shall do!"

To achieve this height of devotion, an executive cannot let his ego think his career or position is his own. Others are affected by his service, and he never knows when he may have to render such service. So, he must take care not to damage his health by overeating or drinking. Neither must he regard a senseless career arrest as his proper end. Much more must he be on his guard against disputes and quarrels with his comrades that may lead to career blows and risk the useless waste of lives in a disloyal and undutiful manner. To this end it is essential for him to think carefully before he speaks, for it is out of words that disputes arise. When disputes grow hot, abuse is apt to follow. And when one executive abuses another, the affair can hardly end amicably. So if there is any risk of a dispute, remember that your life does not belong just to you but also to your company. Control your temper so that the matter goes no further. Such is the duty of a discreet and loyal executive.

Duties

The duties of the executive are twofold, strategic and constructive. When the company is at war, he must be in the office and the field, day and night, evolving strategy without a moment's rest. Construction is necessary as well since implementing strategic "barriers to entry" requires all ranks of employees to build continuously, as fast and as strenuously as possible, the strongholds, moats, and fortified outposts needed to protect the company. These barriers are necessary to make it hard for the competition to duplicate their differentiation or penetrate into home markets to capture the company's customers.

But in peaceful times there is no office duty of the like, and consequently none of the construction connected with it is given due consideration. So, the various types of executives become used to fixed duties regarding operations, management, auditing, control, and the like. To regard these functions as the normal ones for a warrior family and think of field service as nothing but a dream of the past is an error. Then, when it is necessary to assist the CEO in construction by contributing a percentage of their time for meetings, they grudge it and grumble as though it were a distraction. They do not realize that to take part in both strategic and constructive activities is the regular business of executives. So, you find some looking on their ordinary peacetime duties as quite a hardship, and they put in a substitute even when there is nothing the matter with them. Being insensitive to the bother they cause others, they ask them to take their place. Then again, if they are sent out to travel, they resent the fatigue and expense of the journey and put in a substitute for that also, pushing the trouble and expense onto their comrades without being in the least abashed at the contempt they earn. And even if the place to which they are sent is quite near, they complain openly about having to go out twice in one day or else about the unfavorable state of the weather. People who do their duty in this mean spirit, as though it were an imposition, are nothing but embarrassments to the executive position.

The samurai warriors who were born in the age of the civil war of the ancients were always in the field. They were scorched in their armor under the summer skies, pierced through its chinks by the winter blasts, soaked by the rain, cloaked by the snow; they slept on moor and hill with no pillow but their mailed sleeve and ate or drank nothing but unhulled rice and salt soup. And whether they had to fight in the field or had to attack or defend a fortress, they thought it no special hardship or trial, but all in the ordinary day's work. When we reflect on this and how we, born in times of modern civilization and peace, sleep in air conditioning in summer, wrap ourselves in quilts in winter, and eat what we fancy at any time of day, we should indeed consider ourselves lucky. But there is no reason why we should regard our peacetime duties as a serious burden or ignore the importance of strategy development.

CONSIDERATION

It is executive duty to win against competition, destroy obstacles to effectiveness, and support fulfillment and security of all classes of employees in the organization. Thus, even the least of those who bear this title must never commit any violence or injustice against these classes of employees. That is to say, he must not demand any more than is reasonable. Neither should he wear them out by forced service of long hours when they are not satisfied giving up their lives for the inefficient planning and ineffective leadership of their manager.

He must not order articles from suppliers and then neglect to pay them or keep them waiting for their money. One should always be considerate to one's staff, sympathetic to suppliers, and careful they are not ruined. And though you may not at once settle the debts you may have incurred in transactions, you certainly ought to pay something on them from time to time so as not to cause loss and distress. Executives whose duty it is to chastise robbers and thieves must not imitate the ways of these criminals.

TRAVEL

An executive on a journey should travel with important documents and minor toiletries as carry-on baggage. That way, if his checked baggage should fall off a transport en route, he may still carry out his mission. But to check in everything and then arrive at a destination with nothing but the clothes on his back is not good planning. He should put on his baggage an insignia or label of his name and company, so that it may be returned quickly if lost. There must not be the least carelessness about these things. Also, luggage should be of good quality, so that if the company name is seen, it is not disrespectful to the house in which he serves. And when, as is the custom on journeys nowadays, he is riding with a senior official or honored colleague, he should wait to seat himself until after the guest has chosen a seat. And the reason is that if he rushes in to grab a desirable seat, and the other feels constrained by the choice left him, the other may feel embarrassment asking for the favor of switching seats.

In crossing great distances it is always wise to engage transport appropriate for the environment and weather. For if you grudge the expense of a train and think you are an expert driver in the snow, and on the way your car fails to move farther, you will look very foolish. Or if you rely on a taxi, it is best to rent a car to ensure transportation to important meetings in case none is available (unless you are in a city well known for taxi service). Upon renting, it is always wise to spend the extra fee for the express service club because an executive who wastes time with lines and paper forms wastes his mission. This principle of always seeking the shortest way must be kept in mind in everything.

The use of time is especially important because an executive travels great distances, and much time can be spent waiting for arrival or departure. Great executives have mastered the time of waiting and can be seen reading journals, books, and newspapers or even doing work whenever waiting occurs. It is best that an executive carry extra mail or reading material in case an unexpected wait occurs. This way he can carry out his duties without delay and be as productive as if he were back at the company.

HIRING AND PROMOTING

In the civil war period, when battles were continuous, if a samurai was killed after a gallant fight or died of wounds, his lord or commander would, out of regard for his services, allow his son to inherit his position. Now that the empire has changed, feudal inheritances of position are no longer applicable in market-driven environments. However appropriate this may seem, it is still fraught with danger. For the ancients had a foundation of family honor and social discipline to ensure proper succession. Today the criteria are clouded with seniority, experience, performance, friendship, favoritism, and other factors not as solid as honor and discipline. So when a senior executive promotes a junior one based on these qualifications, if the decision is a good one, the senior is very happy. If it is a bad one, the senior should humble himself to the CEO, acknowledge the mistake, and rectify it. For a senior executive to protect and hide a bad situation disgraces the house he serves in and dishonors the CEO. This kind of executive breaks the Code and is not following the Way and should not consider himself to be an executive. On the other hand, if the executive admits the error, then trust is maintained and loyalty served. As an executive himself, the CEO bestows forgiveness and understands the learning that has now been realized.

How much more honorable it is if the junior executive, realizing the situation, takes himself out of the position by requesting reassignment or termination. This is a higher honor in that such an executive displays insight and awareness rare in juniors; but even more so, he offers himself for the good of the organization. A CEO would be foolish to allow such an executive to leave ranks and stop service to the house in some capacity. For when battles ensue, he would best be surrounded by such valor.

When a promotion is about to be bestowed, not after, is the time to prevent these problems. Many embarrassments happen when an executive is promoted based on performance in his current position.

This is a lie. For promotion is best applied when the candidate for the new position has demonstrated capability for the new position, not the former one.[7] These are two different things. Many bodies have been lost because of this mistake. It is even best when peers and subordinates can participate in the decision because they know more than the senior executive does about whether the Code is honored.

Respecting Personnel

One who is an executive should, if he finds in his department matters that do not please him, gain agreement with those he leads by reasonable argument and attempt to correct matters for the better. For trivial issues, though, it is well that he be indulgent and patient and not sweat the insignificant. But if the disposition of those he leads is consistently bad and he considers the department at risk of being no further use to the organization, he may close the department and suggest reallocation or downsizing of the resources. But should he not do this, but keep

7. One of the most common frustrations for CEOs is dealing with executives who are not performing up to expectations. One common example is the CEO who has a VP of sales who does not know how to manage salespeople. When I ask why they were promoted, I am told because they were good salespersons themselves. It comes as a shock when the CEO realizes that being a good salesperson suggests little regarding their ability to manage and lead people.

the department, and then shout at and revile his employees with all sorts of abusive and manipulative expressions, he is behaving as an incompetent "boss" of the old style in the Industrial Age. This is not proper for an executive, but an outrageous thing that only a coward would think of doing.

An employee who has potential to contribute to the corporation and is a professional in his industry would not tolerate being threatened or treated this way by anyone; least of all an incompetent. So, a true indicator of these incompetent executives is the level of employee turnover in their departments. Even though they may carry great excuses for their conditions, they are still suspect. Yet if employees are too weak to act, they may stay, and turnover may not look that bad. But to act like this toward employees who are too weak to know their true power is a thing a brave executive never does. And he who does what a brave man hates and avoids is rightly described as a coward.

THE WORK ENVIRONMENT

An executive who is in service should have his departmental area in as fine a condition as the budget will allow. When a corporation's customers, suppliers, and friends come in to look around, if the appearance of the executive's department is good and has dignity, it will rebound to the credit of the CEO as well as to himself. It is also good for the employees, who must work and spend a significant part of their lives in the environment, to have an area that is pleasant and motivating.

It is important that materials purchased not be extravagant and are able to be rearranged, for in this unsettled world even the CEO must keep in mind the possibility of a siege. Thus, the floors must be leased with low risk, and the ability to sublet be available if costs must be managed down. As with the samurai, executives must be ready to move on a moment's notice and burn or exit their areas in time of emergency. The lightest construction and nothing permanent is of the essence for rapid response to enemy attack. Realizing all this, even in this present peaceful age, an executive who wishes to keep his Way unsullied will certainly not think of his department as a permanent structure or lavish any care on elaborate decoration.

There is also another reason for the ability to rapidly change the department. That is for responding to a reorganization of the company in order to meet an opportunity, or threat, as deemed appropriate. For as the market changes, so will departmental functions. New departments will emerge, and established departments will be altered or dismantled.

That will always be the way in changing markets. Any executive who presents permanence or allows employees to think the same can only be considered lacking in common sense.

WEAPONS AND RESOURCE AVAILABILITY

Every executive who is in service must have a supply of weapons suitable to his means. Every department must have the proper tools, skilled resources, and information weapons to do battle. For if these things must be improvised in a hurry, it will be an obvious sign of carelessness and will provoke contempt. Men who have shown neglect in these areas have been attacked by their own side and suffered loss of career, so there must be no lack of precaution in these things. Shallow are men who hang customer service signs and teamwork posters and yet have not invested in the technology, training, and policies to make these ideals a reality. They are seen by their employees and colleagues as weak and uninspired men, although they see themselves as great. It is ironic that they live until they are killed by their own troops.

So, from fear of being put to public shame, an executive must equip himself and his department properly.

Proving Yourself

When a junior executive wishes to have himself seen as the best, advise him to invest only in areas he can influence and not take on projects that are too big. Though he may be young and agile, to go up against corporate policy that is not willing to accommodate his wishes will result in his being crushed under the weight. And if he takes on too many projects for change, though they may be tolerable while he is young and vigorous, as he grows older they will become too much for him. Even a young man may fall from burnout, with the lightest projects a heavy burden and a hindrance. And if a young man gets known for the weight of his projects and standards, he will find it difficult to give them up when he becomes older and less able to support them. So, it is better for the young executive to take on changes he can influence and to gain support from the greater forces and mentors. As that influence grows from smaller successes, then greater projects for change can be undertaken as more will listen and support these new ideas. For unless the young executive gains majority control of voting stock and can appoint himself CEO, he may lose his spirit and anger others, and in the end accomplish nothing. Sometimes it is better for one to leave and join another camp than remain a broken man where he is not understood or his ideas are not supported.

ESCORT ON NEGOTIATIONS

When an executive in service accompanies his CEO on a negotiation, it is most important that he take care to evaluate the layout of the room, including seating, audio-visual equipment, temperature, and food, so that the CEO is not surprised by any compromising details. Because not all executives honor the Code, he should be alert to any unusual recording devices or other devices of espionage, which may cause a disadvantage or loss of strength in the negotiation. He should also be sure that all information and data the CEO may need to render success are available for his needs. For it is the duty of an executive to be vigilant and careful at all times and to think out how he can render any possible service in the calling to which he is appointed.

PROTECTING THE CEO

When in the course of a business journey a staff member, customer, or supplier starts a dispute and comrades join in the quarrel, whether the CEO should get involved or not depends on how the matter is handled. If the CEO becomes involved, it may be difficult to settle the situation. Remember, it is from below that trouble arises, so be very careful to look after not only yourself but your comrades too.

And advise everybody down to the lowest level to make sure nothing unreasonable occurs.

When you are escorting your CEO to a negotiation and the participants begin exchanging words, you must at once be on the alert at your CEO's side to advise him and see how matters go. Should it be impossible to keep the peace and all have to enter the fray, you must at once remove your CEO from the premises, as nothing but bad PR can come of an emotional situation such as this. At the same time, be ready to draw your own defense and hold your own in the battle.

When you accompany your CEO to a social event, should anything untoward happen while he is there, and it appears that there may be a disturbance, intercede by announcing, "I am So-and-so, an executive of Mr. So-and-so, and as things seem rather anxious, I feel a bit concerned and so I have come to see if there is a problem." Then perhaps the participants will reply, "We don't think there is anything serious, though it is natural you should be anxious. But as your CEO is in no danger, pray set your mind at ease." That being so, everyone will be delighted to hear it. Then you should look to your CEO, and if all is well in his eyes, you should take your leave at once.

Education and Development

EDUCATIONAL RESPONSIBILITY

Since the executive stands at the head of the organization and has the duty of management and leadership, it is incumbent on him to be well educated and to have a wide knowledge of the reason of things. In the period of the Industrial Revolution, the young executive warriors went out to battle to command men and machines for efficient production. There was no time to understand the ways to increase knowledge and wisdom. So whether through their own fault or the fault of their managers' teachings, nothing was done about it. Their whole career was devoted exclusively to the Way of the Industrial Warrior.

Now, however, the empire is different. Though executives should still value efficient production, this is no longer sufficient to sustain the organization in battle. So when the young executive is growing, he should be introduced to the books of strategy, the classics of leadership, and the texts of human performance. He should also be taught humility so that he remembers how to deal with humans and not machines. Then he should be made to practice strategy, organizational change, and empowerment exercises so that he may stumble and contradict himself. These are necessary because it is learning from mistakes that increases humility and diminishes self-importance, thus providing the ability to prepare for the death of ego and arrogance. And this is the way the young executive should bring up his successors in time. There is no excuse for illiteracy in his case, as there was for the warrior of the Industrial Revolution. And successors are not to blame for their lack of education either. From now on, it is entirely due to the neglect and incompetence of their managers who do not really know the way to develop leadership successors.

HISTORY

An executive in service, even the latest hire, much more the veteran, should be sure to make himself well versed in the history of his company. This should include its origin, its past records, and its connections, as well as the deeds of any of its comrades who are distinguished. This he should do by inquiring about them from senior members. For, otherwise, if in the course of conversation with outsiders, he turns out to be ignorant of these matters, even if he is considered a good executive in all other points, he will be held in little esteem.

CONTINUOUS LEARNING

In ancient times it was the custom for executive warriors to become ascetics, and indeed there is much resemblance between the two. For instance, among Zen monks there are those who have the same standing as ordinary employees of corporations. The higher ranks are more or less the equivalent of middle managers. Then again, there are those ascetics who wear uniforms of honor and have authority as do senior management of any organization.

In matters of learning, these ascetics seem to be far superior to ordinary executives. The reason is that they leave their teachers and travel around the country from one monastery to another for study, and so they meet many distinguished scholars and accumulate merits in the practice of meditation and virtue. And when they rise up in the organization and become the abbots of the great temples and monasteries, they are still not the least ashamed to continue their study and research in order that they may be worthy of promotion.

If only upper managers in corporations were so humble as to continue to question their own learnings. But many fear they will be seen as "not-knowing." This fear causes them to defend greatly the illusion of being all-knowing, of having all answers, and of being better than. They see themselves as being smooth enough to carry on the charade. They avoid asking if they are succeeding in the illusion, for fear they may be found out. Many already have been.

I should like to see more asceticism among executives of all levels, especially those who have a good income and a fine quality of life and whose only occupation seems to be to keep a desk chair warm and a suit filled out. For there are those who have not even studied management, much less the strategic research, and they go on passing the months and years idly until their beards grow white and their heads bald. Because they have the illusion of aged wisdom, they sometimes assume a new office where they should act as an executive. However, they are so incompetent in their duties, they need the assistance of a colleague or subordinate to carry them out. Or should they be sent to some other department or division, they become so flustered and distracted by preoccupations for the journey that when they do take up their duties, they are barely able to carry them out. They must rely on instructions from seniors and borrow books of reference. This state of things cannot be considered the proper way.

For the duties of the executive are similar among all, and he should consider these duties when he has time. When he meets with officers of capacity and experience, he should cease idle talk and learn from them about matters on which he anticipates he will need advice. He must acquaint himself with all the facts and collect and copy relevant books and plans so he is well informed about his duty at all points. Thus, whatever he is ordered to do at any time he will find easy to undertake. If you depend on others to help you perform your duties, this may do for ordinary issues but, in the rare case when something unusual happens, you may not be able to get any assistance. Then, for good or evil, you must depend on your own ability to solve the problem.

As a senior executive, you must also know such things as who the competition is, where they are strong, where they are weak, where to best position the organization, and what the probability for victory is. From ancient times this office has been regarded as a difficult one. If you should make a miscalculation, the matter most likely will end only in blame for you because you have the control of the troops and are responsible for the lives and families of the company.

It is a most reprehensible thing that men should disgrace these high commands by swaggering in them without any proper knowledge or capacity. It is as though a Zen monk neglected his learning but was promoted because of the virtue of a bald head, and would wear the honored robes of a top rank and hold authority over his brethren. Such an unworthy monk of this type would find himself the laughingstock of the whole community. He would be put to public shame and have to resign so that he would do no special harm to the order. But it is very different with executives who are promoted to similar high offices and are incompetent to lead, for they hide more easily in politics and status quo. They jeopardize the lives of all under them, and the loss they can cause is very great. Even though all under them know who they are, they themselves are ignorant of the fact. On the contrary, they think of themselves as great leaders and do not see the damage they cause to those they lead. They blame any shortcomings on others and on circumstances. Some of these incompetent executives die by unseen hands of those smitten by their incompetence. Others die from an alert board of directors. Still others live on.

It is essential, therefore, that executives behave as ascetics and study whenever they have time. They must gain a thorough knowledge of ordinances and battle, for both study and practice are most necessary to one who holds a high leadership position. In this they must be very diligent.

THE MANAGEMENT ARTS

One who is an executive, even though a junior one, should provide himself with a suitable instructor or mentor in order to study the management arts. This is to ensure he will know all there is to be known on the subject. Some may say this is not at all necessary for a minor executive, but this I consider a very shallow view. In all ages there have been a number of executives who have risen from quite humble positions to make a name as great leaders and to become heads of large companies and countries. And even now I do not think it impossible for a minor manager to become head of a great division. Moreover, the study of management arts will make one who is naturally clever more so, and one who is born somewhat dull rather less so. Therefore, all executives ought certainly to apply themselves to finding a mentor or instructor in these arts.

A bad use, however, can be made of this study in order to puff up one's ego and disparage one's colleagues by a lot of high-flown but incorrect arguments that only mislead the young and spoil their spirit. For an executive of this kind gives forth a wordy discourse that may appear to be correct and proper enough, but he is only striving for effect and thinking of his own advantage. So, the result is the deterioration of his character and the loss of the real executive spirit, and he will usually be unaware of this even if he is found out by his subordinates to be a fake. This is a fault arising from a superficial study of the subject. Those who begin this study should never be satisfied to go only halfway, but persevere until they understand all its secrets. Only then should they return to their people to apply the art. But if people spend a lot of time in this study and get only halfway and are quite unable to master it, they may not be able to regain their former effectiveness, but lapse into a confused state that is most unfortunate.[8] Even then, however, they must not puff themselves up with fashionable words of the latest management theories. There is an old saying that bean sauce that smells of bean sauce is not good, and so it is with the management pedants.

8. The fashion waves of management theories that splash across the shelves of bookstores every month can drown the most well-intentioned executive. Mastery of any particular one, especially one that may in fact be able to produce bottom-line results, is difficult. While most organizational changes fail, managers and consultants are remarkably silent. Industry data reveal Total Quality Management failure rates as high as 73 percent, restructuring failures over 65 percent, and only slight to moderate success in implementing teams, with only 17 percent working well. Even reengineering is coming under fire. For an executive to act as an expert places him or her on dangerous ground. The true learning of success is a painful and risky proposition that only great leaders can endure—and usually with great mentors.

INFORMATIONSHIP

In ancient times all executive knights, high and low, considered archery and horsemanship as the first of the military arts. Later they added the practice of swordsmanship. Today executives must be trained in the use of weapons of the twenty-first century. The most powerful of these weapons are information-based and in the form of machines that gather, carry, and manipulate data. Informationship, the mastery of these weapons, is essential in carrying out battles in the marketplace.

There are many ways to teach information-ship, as there were many to teach horsemanship to the ancient ones. One means is in learning how to apply information devices inside products of the company. The implanting of such devices dramati-cally increases value to customers and deals a serious blow to the enemy. Examples of these weapons can already be seen in new products, even commodi-ties—washing machines, toilets, and ovens, as well as manufacturing tools, cars, and phones. It enables a more effective use of the product in improving profitability or quality of life.

Another method is in teaching how to link information channels to the customer so the cus-tomer becomes intrinsically attached to the organi-zation in a meaningful way, and thus the value of service is improved. By allowing customers to access company services intimately and conveniently, defenses are strengthened and many enemy attacks are blocked. An executive cannot sleep even under the most protected walls, since the enemy is always innovating new ways of penetration. Understanding and responding to customer needs through these linkages requires constant vigilance. Learning this art well can keep the enemy locked out or severely delayed in attack.

Training is also essential in the use of information devices inside the organization to improve processes and functions, and linkages between them. This dramatically increases the organization's ability to serve. Samurai communication among distant outposts and with the central lord allowed effective support and competitive response to threats to the empire. Executives should learn how to institute the modern version of these systems. All classes of employees are valuable in battle, and so all stations should have access to any relevant information needed to perform valiantly.

Finally, young and older executives must be trained in the application of information weapons not only in strategy but also in personal use. They need to be educated constantly about the machines and instruments available, as these change rapidly and enemies seek to exploit these new weapons as quickly as possible. Those that resist this education are at risk, just as ancient samurai who could not ride well or shoot arrows straight or throw spears accurately failed in battle. They not only lost their lives but cost their organizations many lives as well. These executives failed to accommodate the skills necessary to win. Even though they may have been protected by more skilled colleagues, when it came time for them to be accounted for on their own merit, they were unable to perform. Executives such as these become an embarrassment and react by defending themselves with memories of past greatness, when they had mastered things that are no longer useful in the battles of the day.

Executive Knowledge

In the Way of the Executive there are two knowledge bases—the *organizational* and the *strategic*. The *organizational* is divided into the two sections of the "executive" and the "staff," while the *strategic* is similarly divided into those of "formulation" and "implementation." As to the "executive" section of the *organizational* base, all executives must maintain appropriate leadership and managerial style, including how they present themselves to the employees. Ancient samurai would take a hot bath, do their hair with their foreheads properly shaved, and always wear the ceremonial dress appropriate to the occasion, including two swords as well as a fan in their girdles. Today's executive must also dress in an appropriate manner, whether casually or formally. When he receives a guest, he must treat him with the etiquette due his rank and must refrain from idle political talk. Even in having lunch or a drink, it must be done correctly without slovenliness and with no lack of vigilance for a positive attitude. If he is serving in some capacity when he is off duty, he must not lounge about doing nothing but should read and practice his education, storing his mind with the ancient history and precepts of other warrior houses. He should, in short, conduct himself at all times with manners proper to an executive.

Next comes the section on "staff." This concerns recruiting, exercising, and developing the skills of people necessary for producing results. Just as fencing, spear practice, horsemanship, and shooting with the bow used to be important, today the skills are those of communication, problem-solving, teamwork, meeting management, self-discipline, continuous improvement, and all else that pertains to the technical mastery of the position. These must be enthusiastically studied and practiced so that all will be disciplined and resolute. If these two dimensions of the "executive" and the "staff" are well understood, the *organizational* knowledge base may be considered complete, and this would appear to most people to be sufficient for the stockholders and board.

But an executive is also an official for *strategic* situations. When the organization is in a state of disorder or under competitive threat, the executive must serve the CEO by ensuring that the armor and arms are on hand to advance into enemy market territory. It is the various methods of arranging matters on such a campaign that are known as the rule of "formulation" of the strategy, and this is a thing that must be known. Then comes the rule of "implementation," which is the method of handling the staff when they come into contact with the enemy to give battle—changing the organization, its weapons, and its products appropriately. And if things go according to plan, there is victory; and if not, there is defeat. This too is a thing the secrets of which must be understood.

And what is called a first-class executive is one who is skilled in all four sections of these two knowledges. To be experienced in only the two sections of the *organizational* may be sufficient for the duties of the average manager, but one who is ignorant of the *strategic* sections can never become a high officer. It is therefore most important that all executives should consider and realize they cannot rise to the highest position without profound study of the *strategic* knowledge.

Leadership

Avoid Being an Oppressor

Executives serving under superiors have to put up with being attentive to them and at the same time be tolerant of their unequal qualities. But should they have the good fortune to be promoted or given charge of a company themselves, they should be sympathetic and considerate of those under them while also fulfilling their duty to their CEO. It is perhaps unnecessary to say they should not be partial or flattered, but if in course of time they should rise in their positions, they need to be aware that their former attitude may be apt to change. For instance, are there not executives who were admirable when they were humble managers but who deteriorated when they rose to high office and so were discarded by their CEO and ruined? Beware of self-importance and the seduction of power. Those under you have eyes to see and do not like to be treated in a manner that you too resented when you were in their position.

Avoid Extortion

For an executive in service, the duties connected with the treasury are the most difficult. With ordinary knowledge and ability it is a great problem how to do well for one's stockholders without causing some hardship to employees, not to speak of suppliers or customers. If you think only of your stockholders' short-term interests, you mortgage the future and the employees will have much to put up with. Yet if you try only to make employees comfortable, stockholders will not be so well off. So, there is sure to be some deficiency somewhere. Also, however clever and shrewd an executive may be by nature, the disease of covetousness is easy to catch. If he has control over arrangements in the accounting of profits and expenses, he may ignore consequences and seek luxury by scheming to embezzle his company's money. Thus he will build a big house, buy a fancy car, and collect curios to make an elegant appearance. This is the sort known as a thieving executive.

There is another type of executive, however, who makes a new system different from that of the former, asserting that it is for his CEO's benefit, without caring what hardship it causes his colleagues. It makes employees suffer unfair expense reductions, so they cannot work productively, and customer service declines so that he increases profit without any regard for the immediate future or people's comfort. Also he may deceive the board so that they agree to grant him improper increases in salary and rewards. But should these new regulations prove unworkable and ineffective, he will represent them as having been planned by others and so avoid punishment by sheltering behind their backs. This sort is known as the cheating executive.

Now as to the previously mentioned thieves, as they steal in a way unworthy of an executive and pervert justice accordingly, when heaven's punishment falls on them and the fact is made manifest by their personal ruin, the matter is ended. When these executives are themselves overthrown, people are no longer oppressed, and the trouble in the administration and loss to the company also ceases. But the cheating executive produces a much more extensive injury that is more difficult to repair. For damage to the administration of the company is the greatest possible crime, even if personal greed and embezzlement are not involved. Therefore do the sages of old declare that it is better to have a thieving official than a cheating one. Though for an executive there can be nothing worse than to gain the reputation of an embezzler, the ancients condemn the cheater more. So if the thief is punished by firing, the cheater ought to be prosecuted. This may have been the judgment of former times. In the present day, however, since the actions of both may be regarded as the same, namely feathering their nest under the pretense of working for their CEO's benefit, both are considered as equally heinous criminals. And for such a great offense it is difficult to say what penalty is adequate.

AVOID ABUSING POWER AND AUTHORITY

An executive in service may be said to borrow his CEO's authority, be lent such authority, or steal it. For instance, when a young executive holds an important office, he may be embarrassed by social customs or the current fashion and have to carry out his duties by relying upon his CEO's authority. He thus borrows his authority by deferring to his CEO's name. If with its assistance he carries out his CEO's intentions and benefits the people, he will have used it rightly in doing his duty with proper circumspection. But if, when he finds his comrades and outsiders treating him with respect and addressing him as "Mr." and other signs of power, he becomes greedy of dignity and loath to part with it, then he may abuse such power and be described as one who steals it.

Then there is the situation when the CEO is found lending his authority and giving his prestige to executives for temporary situations such as when the CEO is away, or for special projects. Although the executives are required to give back this authority when the task is finished, sometimes from an easygoing nature the CEO allows them to keep it for some time. But when some incident arises that requires it be given back, the recipients make it difficult and costly. Here the executive certainly robs his CEO of his authority. This is not only a great disgrace to a CEO but causes him great damage.

If any one executive gets too much power, that of the CEO is thereby decreased. And if people come to think they can get what they want by honoring the executive because he controls all access to the CEO, they will think only of getting into his good graces and regard the CEO as of secondary importance. Thus, the benevolent relations of CEO and executive disappear, and loyal executives will become conspicuous by their absence. Should some emergency arise, there will be no good men left to deal with it. Moreover, not only outside executives but those in the central office will be oppressed by the authority of such a person. This will cause them to shrink in on themselves, and this also is not good for their CEO. For they will say nothing about things they ought to notice but only regret it in their hearts and grumble privately to their friends, without anybody standing up and reporting it to their CEO. The arbitrary conduct and partiality of the offender, and the extent of his honor and glory, remain unknown to his CEO, who only thinks well of all he does and thus by negligence brings about great misfortune. And the incapacity to know who people are is generally condemned as unbefitting a chief executive.

Moreover, a man of this sort who cares nothing about what his CEO thinks is not likely to be sensitive to the opinion of his comrades. He will favor the little officials and give those who are his friends and acquaintances fees and bribes from corporate property, while taking their return presents for himself. When he entertains his guests, he has the meals, liquor, and desserts bought from his company credit card. So, acting on the principle that what is my CEO's is mine and what is mine is my own, he weakens his CEO's estate and causes him great loss. Think over all this very deeply therefore and remember always to be humble and suppress all pretensions when granted any privilege by your CEO, so that nothing may dim the brightness of the company. As the ancient saying has it, the loyal retainer does not realize his own existence but only that of his lord.

Do Not Defile the Executive Position

There is a saying that officials and white garments are best when new. Though but a joke, I think it is true. For a white shirt is very beautiful when new, but after it has been worn for some time the collar and sleeves get soiled, ring-around-the-collar sets in, and it begins looking very unpleasant. So too officials when they are fresh and inexperienced are very motivated and pay attention to the slightest detail. They respect the oaths and penalties they take on themselves and fear to transgress accordingly. So they serve without greed or dishonesty and are spoken well of by all their clan.

After officials have been in office a long time, however, they are apt to presume on people's obedience, develop a big opinion of themselves, and do uncivil things they would never have done previously. Further, when they were new to office they would not accept favors that might cause them to feel indebted or that might seem a conflict of interest, as the oath of the service requires. Or should there be some special reason why they must receive them, before long they would make a return of equal value, so there was a win-win situation. After a while, however, a covetous spirit begins to arise in them. And while still declaring they will take nothing and make an honest appearance, it is somehow made known that this is only a political ruse. Soon their apparent scruples are overcome, and they accept these favors. To return the favor, they cannot but help rob the company or give partial decisions.

This defilement is just like the dirty color of a white garment. The difference, however, is that this dirt can be washed away with lye, whereas the stain on a man's heart gets so ingrained that it can hardly be removed. It is enough to wash a garment every week, but a man's heart has to be continually cleansed and rinsed, when both sleeping and waking, every day of the year without remission—especially when it is easily soiled. Just as lye and the practice of using it are needed for garments, so is the practice of Integrity, Bravery, and Honor also needed in cleansing the hearts of executives. For some may compromise these values, and though you may apply loyalty or duty, there is some dirt so ingrained that it will not be washed out even then. But if to these things be added valor and intense application to their use, then the defilement can be removed entirely. And this is the most profound secret of the purification of the executive heart.

GIVING AND RECEIVING FAVORS

Anyone who receives special attention from his CEO, such as a personal gift or special time after work for a sport or a drink, should be careful. If he accepts the gift or attention, he should not boast or seek to be obvious, and, if necessary, should be clear with others about his intention. Otherwise, he may give the impression of "sucking-up," and this would be impolite and not good form for an executive. Also, when these favors are accepted, he should not expect special future consideration, as this would be disrespectful.

In addition, when any of your colleagues or staff is either very ill or suffering from some bereavement, even though you may not be very intimate with him, you should take care not to place any pressure or expectation on him and give orders to your staff to do likewise. This is not only because of what they may think but to avoid the shame of being despised by colleagues and staff as mannerless.

FAMILY BUSINESS

Usually among our families, members are treated as brothers, sisters, aunts, uncles, nephews, nieces, mothers, and fathers should be. We accommodate their personalities and differences by changing how we address, tolerate, and revolve our lives within the context of the family. But with executives, it is not the same. Family behavior is not necessarily appropriate in business. The purpose of business is to win customers, but some families use business to provide a field for dysfunctional family behavior. It is well that family members decide where to draw the line between family and business.

In the case where family members are both owners and employees, it is especially essential for them to understand the difference between employee and owner—an owner's role is different from an employee's role. One can still be an owner yet not be employed by the organization. Conversely, one can be an employee and not an owner. It is best not to confuse the two, and to understand which role you are in when you are speaking. Good family owners who are also executives realize this and, given the priority of the business, remove themselves from the organization when they realize they are getting in the way. Family executives should jealously guard against family issues negatively affecting the company. Only those of tremendous ego will fail to see the difference and thus will risk the business to support their own egos' pride. This they do because they do not keep death firmly in mind. If family relations are strong, the business will have an advantage against the competition. If they are weak, the business will be at a disadvantage and much energy will be wasted on issues and concerns that have nothing to do with serving and winning customers. Whichever the case, this will readily be seen by the employees.

Most times it is helpful to bring in an outside mediator to help the family see its role. For in usual family matters, members are met and soon left, to be seen again only on special occasions. But in business, relations cannot be left and seen again later but must be seen constantly day by day. This increases the possibility of family dysfunction infecting the business. If things deteriorate, good executives will hire outside leaders to run the organization while members remove themselves to be a family again. Or they will evolve a level of relationship that allows them to behave as executives without feeling personally attacked. Many good families have been destroyed by their participating in a business together. The Way of the Executive should not allow the business to affect filial duty, or vice versa.

The Latter End

The executive, whether senior or junior, has to set before all other things the consideration of how to meet his inevitable end. However clever or capable he may have been, if his ego or quest for power causes him upset and dishonor when a hard decision must be made for the good of the business, he will make a poor showing when he comes to face it all. His previous good deeds will be forgotten, and all decent people will despise him, so that he will be covered with shame.

For when an executive goes out to battle and valiantly and splendidly wins in the markets and makes himself a legend in the company, it is only because he made up his mind to die. He is always prepared for death of the ego or body. And if unfortunately the worst happens, and his company is captured by an enemy investor and he must lose his position or employment in the company, he must leave with dignity. When his opponent asks for his resignation, he must declare it at once loudly and clearly and yield up his head with honor and without the slightest sign of fear. Or should he be so badly wounded that he is demoted and no one can do anything for him, the proper procedure for an executive is to answer to his superior officers and comrades in his best form without anger or spite. Or if he feels he is mortally wounded, then he should make an end without more ado.

Similarly, in times of peace if he is found to be incompetent as a senior, but no less if he is young, he ought to show firmness and resolution and attach no importance to leaving the company. Naturally if he is in high office, but also however low his position may be, he should request the presence of his superior and inform him of his intention. He should state that although he has long enjoyed his employment and has fervently carried out his duties with all his power, unfortunately he has now realized the serious limitation of his ability to lead. He also knows it will be difficult to recover. Consequently, he wishes to resign and to express his gratitude for past kindness and trusts and to be remembered respectfully when future employers call for reference. This done, he should say farewell to his friends and colleagues. He should explain to them that it is not the business of an executive to die quickly after receiving great favors of the company and their companionship but that unfortunately, in his case, it is unavoidable. He should tell those who are young that they must carry on his intentions and firmly resolve to do their duty for the customer, ever increasing this passion so as to serve with all the vigor they possess. Should they fail to do this or act in any disloyal or undutiful way, then even from the career beyond he will disown and disinherit them. Such is the leave-taking of a true executive.

And in the words of the sage too, it is written that when a man is about to die, his words should be of right honor. This is what the end of an executive should be, and how different it is from one who refuses to regard his unavoidable end and is worried about dying. His ego is too strong, and death of ego can be as fearful as death of body. It is this type of person who rejoices if people tell him he is great and dislikes it if they say he is not performing. All the while he fusses, making himself look good, and busies himself in a constant state of useless activity. As his career performance gradually worsens, he does not say anything to anyone but ends up bungling the one career death he has, so that it is no better than that of a dog or cat. This is because he does not keep death always before his eyes as I recommended he do in my first chapter, but puts any mention of it away from him as ill omened. He seems to think he will live forever, hanging on to existence with a greedy intensity. His arrogance and self-importance avoid death at all costs. One who goes into battle in this cowardly spirit is not likely to die a glorious death in a halo of honor. So one who values the executive ideal should see to it that he knows how to die properly.